# Love, Pain, and Shame

Rachel Ermutlu

BookLeaf Publishing

India | USA | UK

Presentation by *BookLeaf Publishing*

Web: www.bookleafpub.com

E-mail: info@bookleafpub.com

ISBN: 9789360946814

First edition 2024

*For my wonderful husband, Dan*

*Thank you for loving me through all of my
struggles*

# ACKNOWLEDGEMENT

First and foremost, I want to thank God. I want to thank Him for saving me from myself when I was suicidal and for all the opportunities and blessings He has given me since then. I'd like to thank my husband, Dan for supporting me in whatever I am doing. Finally, I'd like to thank Bookleaf Publishing for helping me publish this book.

# PREFACE

In 2019, I was diagnosed with Obsessive Compulsive Disorder (OCD). I was 29 and I had been having scary, intrusive thoughts since I was 19. I thought OCD was being very organized and liking things clean. I'm not organized and I am a fairly messy person so I never thought I had OCD. That's not what OCD is. It's having scary thoughts come into your head and trying to do things to get the thoughts to go away. The poems about OCD are part of my story (some of the other poems are just made up). I want to let people know it is okay to be honest about your mental health struggles. If you share with someone you will learn you are not alone.

# Beautiful Disaster

She feels so unworthy of love
Why would these thoughts pop into her brain?
She wears her shame like a glove
Why is she in so much pain?
Pain is not what she is after
Why is there so much shame?
She is a lovely, beautiful disaster

# Beauty

What is it?
Who decides what is beautiful
And what is not?
You can have a pretty face
But an ugly soul
Beauty runs deeper than the surface
So much deeper

# Age is Beauty

You are so beautiful
Your years of wisdom make you glow
Makeup is not needed
To see your radiant beauty
It can be accentuated
But your beauty has not faded

# Beauty From Ashes

Have you felt crazy?
Have you felt depressed?
Even if you are very blessed
Have you struggled with a mental illness?
Hoping for just a little stillness
Have you felt ugly on the inside and out?
Do compliments cause you to doubt?
Have you struggled with hating yourself?
Feeling like you are beyond help
No matter what you've been through
There's a God who loves you
Remember to have self-compassion
You are truly beauty from ashes

# Love

5

When two souls become one
When it feels so good to run
Into the arms of each other
You feel there could never be another
Who you love this much
Your heart beats faster with every touch
When this love is true
You never stop saying, 'I love you'

# The Pain of Love

When you love someone
Their pain is your pain
Their sorrow is your sorrow
You wish for them a better tomorrow
It hurts your heart to see them hurting
You badly wish you could carry their burden
You don't need to make their pain your own
Just let them know they're not alone

# Always Loved

If you have depression
You are loved
If you've faced oppression
You are loved
When you have intrusive thoughts
You are loved
Even if you hate your guts
You are loved
When you struggle to like yourself
You are loved
When you wish you were someone else
You are loved
If you have anxiety
You are loved
When your flaws are all you see
You are loved
No matter how you feel
You are loved
God's love for you is real
You are ALWAYS loved

# The Abyss

She wonders if she is enough
Many made her feel unloved
She thinks maybe if I give a little more
This man won't leave like those before
She craves so much attention
She wonders if there's an invention
To cure her loneliness
Is she the only one like this?
She feels the loss of her innocence
As slowly, she falls into the abyss

# The Monster

The monster in your brain
Causes so much pain
The monster's not you
It's kind of like the flu
Except it might not go away
Your monster's here to stay
It can be shrunk in size
Therapy saves so many lives
Medication need not cause shame
It can help so much with the pain
You can have a breakthrough
The monster can be almost invisible to you

# Real OCD

Intrusive thoughts are very scary
Especially when you've never heard of them
before
They made me not want to live anymore
I made a plan to kill myself
And wished that I was someone else
I couldn't leave my husband and son
So I looked up how to make the thoughts be
gone
I was diagnosed with OCD
Which didn't make any sense to me
I have a messy car and house
I share food with my son and spouse
I'm an unorganized non-clean freak
How could I have OCD?
I want to make people more aware
So we don't have to live in despair
I'm managing with Prozac and therapy
The symptoms of my OCD
My husband, therapy, and medication
Helped me realize I don't need a permanent
vacation
My husband is supportive of me
Without him I don't know where I'd be
I'm so glad I am his wife

Or I may have taken my life
I'm feeling so much better now
And you can, too if you are shown how
I'm learning how to be me
While living with my OCD

# Will I?

OCD is a debilitating disorder
It's not just about keeping your house in order
It's having thoughts get stuck in your head
Will I hurt someone?
Will I cheat on the one I love?
Will I contaminate them if I don't wear a glove?
I better end my life before I hurt someone
It's the only way to keep them safe from what's
to come
No!
There is help for all your strife
Please don't end your life
There is medication and therapy
To help you be the best that you can be
You are not a bad person, you have OCD

# Brave

OCD is not a personality quirk
It's wondering if you are subconsciously a jerk
It's not just about hating the mess
It's wondering if your thoughts should be
confessed
OCD is not and adjective
It's wondering if you deserve to live
It's obsessing over scary thoughts
And wondering if the fight is lost
The fight is not lost
There are good and bad days
You can win, just try to be brave

# Intrusive

I had intrusive thoughts for at least ten years
Before I learned that's what they were
I hated myself oh so much
I thought should I jump in front of a truck?
I prayed for the thoughts to go away
But they seemed to be here to stay
I couldn't tell anyone
No-one could know
If they find out they'll tell me to go
I believed I deserved to rot in hell
The thoughts and my morals did not gel
My attempts to repress made them worse
I thought that maybe I was cursed
I became extremely suicidal
Didn't care for my own survival
I finally decided to tell someone
You have OCD, you're not the only one
They gave me medication and therapy
And I'm managing my OCD

# Lies

Intrusive thoughts
Negative thoughts
Thoughts that tell you what you're not
Or is it maybe what you are?
Stupid
Worthless
Crazy
Horrible
Unlovable
And so much more
These are all lies
Please, open your eyes
You are not your thoughts
The fight can be fought
I know your pain is real
It is possible to heal
No matter what you do
You are the best at being you

# Hidden

Hiding behind a tree
Hoping no-one sees me
Thinking if I show my face
I will be a huge disgrace
I don't want to be a burden
Even if I'm really hurting
My problems are too small
To bother anyone at all
Talking to a therapist
Would be way too selfish
I need to care for everyone else
It's selfish to take care of myself
This is not true
Make sure to take care of you
Self-care is essential
Don't keep your struggles confidential
You need to take care of yourself
To have strength for everyone else

# It Gets Better

Do you ever feel like you're in so much pain?
Wondering if you'll be happy again
Thinking it would be easier to end it all
I'm here to tell you that's not the right call
There are so many reasons to live
Here, let me give you a list
When you feel unlovable
There's a God whose love's unfathomable
He can help you
With what you're going through
There are many people in your life
Who'd be so sad if you took your life
There are so many loving faces
Help can be found in many places
Please, don't write that letter
Trust me, it does get better

# Mirrors

Have you ever looked in a mirror
And wondered why you are here?
Have you looked at your face with disgust
And wondered if you should just
Kill yourself
Wanting to be someone else
Hating the face you see
Feeling so ugly
Wishing to be twenty pounds thinner
Thinking will I ever look like her?
Mirrors sometimes tell us lies
You are definitely a prize
We are all works of art
But what matters is your heart

# Not the End



Have you ever wanted your story to end?
Are you sick of always having to pretend?
Mental health struggles are a real thing
Don't let others say you are just faking
Mental health is physical health, too
Your brain is a physical part of you
Don't be afraid to ask for help
Many people want to help you get well
You don't have to pretend
Please, don't let your story end

# No Shame

Have you ever been buried in shame?
Feeling you deserve the pain
You've been going through
Believing the lies are true
Obsessing over past mistakes
Thinking you don't deserve grace
Thinking you're the only one
Has this only just begun?
We all struggle with shame
You are not always to blame
No matter how you feel
God's grace and love are real

# Addiction

Just one more
Won't hurt
You say
Again
And again
And again
More
And
More
And more of yourself
You give
To the drugs
or sex
or alcohol
or maybe even something else
You say
I can stop
Whenever I want
You say
No-one's getting hurt
This quite simply is not true
You're not only hurting others
But also you

# You Matter!

22

Living with depression can be hard
You might be afraid to let down your guard
Don't be afraid to get help if you need
Don't wait until you can no longer breathe
You're not the only one who feels this way
You wonder if depression is here to stay
Don't give up, there is hope
I've found many different ways to cope
Should I live or die you say
Is this really the only way?
Please don't do the latter
I want to let you know you matter!